The Family
Christmas
Book

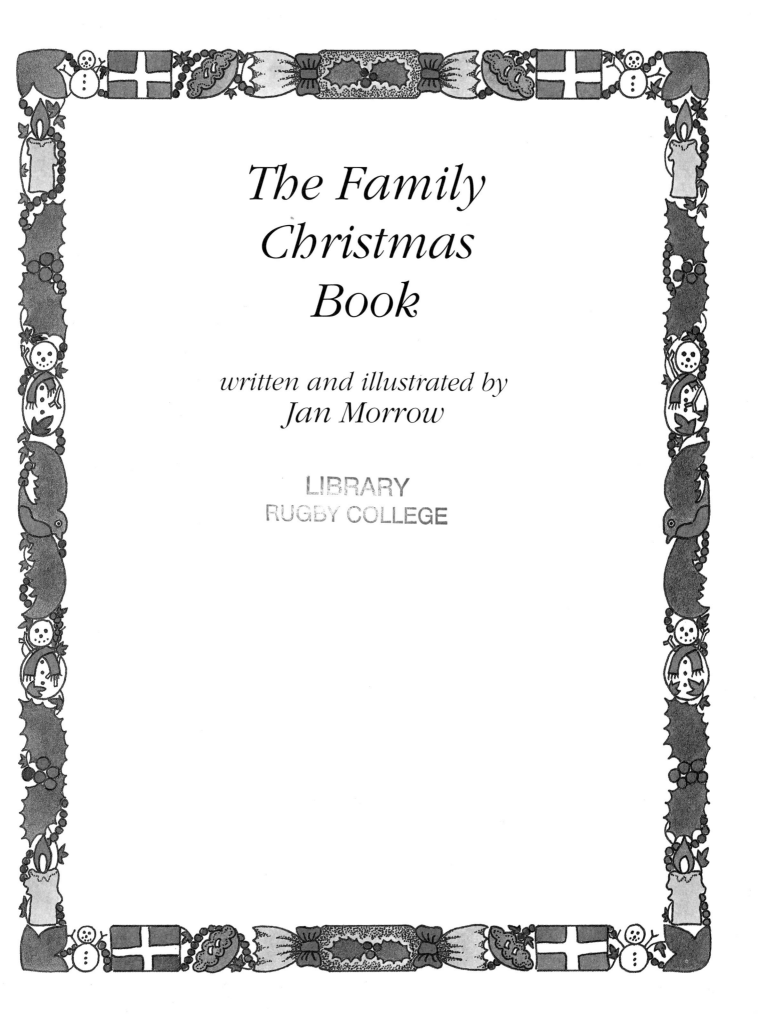

The Family Christmas Book

written and illustrated by
Jan Morrow

LONGMAN GROUP UK LIMITED

Longman House
Burnt Mill, Harlow, Essex CM20 2JE, England
and Associated Companies throughout the World

First published 1990

British Library Cataloguing in Publication Data
Morrow, Jan
    The family Christmas book.
    I. Christmas activities
    I. Title
    790.1

    ISBN 0-582-04431-6
Set in 9/9 pt Frutiger, 45 Linotron 202

Produced by Longman Group (FE) Ltd
Printed in Hong Kong

Contents

Introduction

Whatever our religious beliefs, it is certain that many people find the 'modern' Christmas with its blatant commercialism rather disappointing and empty. Even the traditional symbols of Christmas have lost their meaning and are displayed without any thought to their place in the Christmas story.

With the help of this book you can re-establish a truly 'traditional' Christmas. You will find out about the history of the Christmas symbols and traditions, and the background to the introduction of each one; then you will find suggestions for using them in creative and original activities with your family.

Many of our Christmas symbols are truly international and each country produces a slightly different variation on the same theme.

'The Family Christmas Book' introduces some of the best Christmas ideas from around the globe.

This is first and foremost a family book. The activities are designed to reintroduce many of the older customs of the festive season and present them in ways which will involve the whole family. There are six sections in the book. The first contains lots of different ideas to help you prepare for Christmas. The following sections deal with Christmas Eve, Christmas Day, Boxing day, New Year's Eve, and finally Twelfth Night. This book will guide you through the complete Christmas period.

In these days of the plastic Father Christmas and wall-to-wall television, the family rarely joins together in a creative activity at Christmas time. Decorations, cards and presents are usually bought from shops; games and entertainment are provided ready-made by the TV.

'The Family Christmas Book' provides dozens of inventive ideas based on truly traditional customs which will involve your family and help them to make the most of their time together at Christmas.

The History of Christmas

The exact date of Christ's birth has never been established. At the end of the third century Christians were celebrating his birth on different dates and it was not until 350 AD when Pope Julius the First declared that December the 25th was 'The Day' that most Western churches accepted the now traditional date.

Pope Julius chose his date wisely. It happens to coincide quite effectively with various winter festivals which were already celebrated by the people at that time of the year. By choosing December 25th the Christian Church was able to absorb rather than suppress a variety of established pagan celebrations and traditions. The Romans had used December 25th to mark the birth of the Sun God Mithras. On January 1st tribute had been paid to their Goddess Strenia and evergreen branches were given as gifts. In Northern Europe the winter solstice of December 21st was traditionally the feast of Yule and Yule logs were burnt at this time in tribute to the gods Thor and Odin.

So by selecting December as Christ's birthday the Christian church has been able to incorporate many of the customs and traditions which were formerly associated with the ancient myths and legends of the people. But why the 25th? The 25th of March was the Pagan festival of Spring and the church had adopted that day for Gabriel's visit to Mary. Nine months from March 25th gives you the date of December 25th.

During the middle ages Christmas became undoubtedly the most popular festival of the year. However its pagan associations were frowned upon by the Puritans and finally Christmas was banned by Oliver Cromwell's government. The celebration was only revived after the restoration of the monarchy in 1660.

Since that date the main focus of the celebration has become increasingly domestic. The festival has also become shorter. It used to continue right up to February 2nd which is Candlemas day. Perhaps the element of family sentimentality reached a peak during the reign of Victoria when romantic nostalgia and the ideal of family life was promoted by the monarchy.

Certainly many of our current Christmas card images and ideas of the magic of Christmas seem to reflect back to the Victorian age.

Preparing for Christmas

Advent

The four weeks leading up to Christmas are referred to as Advent. Christians believe that the weeks represent the coming of Christ and the fourth week is never completed in order to symbolise the idea that Christ's coming will never end.

Advent used to be associated with a period of fasting before the feast and it has always been a period of preparation for the Christmas festivities.

During Advent, in the period before the Reformation, priests from the local church would take models of the Virgin Mary and the baby Jesus round to houses in order to collect money. The half penny paid for this favour was said to bring the household good luck for the next twelve months.

St Nicholas's day is also celebrated during Advent on December 6th. In Britain and America St Nicholas's day and Christmas day have been amalgamated but in Switzerland, Holland, Germany and in many Catholic countries, children hang up their stockings on St Nicholas's Eve in order to receive their presents.

We now associate Advent with Advent crowns and calendars. The tradition of marking the passing of Advent with a crown seems to have started in Germany, where a wreath made from pine branches was traditionally suspended from the ceiling by ribbons and the four candles on it were lit on each Sunday during Advent. Lighting these candles not only symbolised the passing of time before Christ's coming but was also thought to ward off evil spirits.

More recently, Advent Calendars have become popular and children can mark the passing of the four weeks before Christmas by discovering a tiny picture or gift each day.

🐦 An Advent candle crown 🐦

This pretty hanging crown can look extremely attractive.

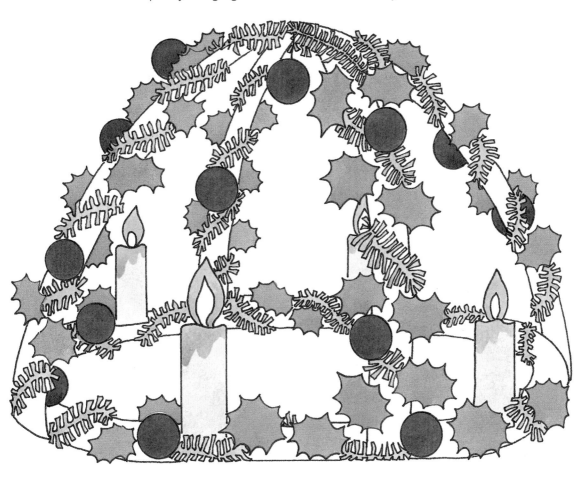

1 Take a sheet of thick coloured card and cut out a ring (30cm wide), and two long strips of card (50cm by 3cm).

2 Using the illustration as a guide, bend the strips over the top of the ring to form a dome and glue the strips into position by folding 1cm of each strip under the ring.

3 With a sharp pair of scissors make four small (2cm) slits in the ring between each of the strips of card.

4 Decorate the dome with some tinsel, cut out paper holly leaves, and a few baubles. Attach a loop of string or ribbon to the top of the dome.

5 Finally, cut out and colour four card candles 8cm high by 2cm wide and add one of these candles to the dome on each of the four Sundays during Advent by standing the base of the candle in one of the slits in the ring.

❧ An Advent King's crown ❧

This particular Advent crown is likely to prove very popular with children.

1 From a strip of coloured card 60cm by 10cm, cut out a pattern along one edge and sellotape the strip into a crown shape.

2 Decorate the crown with 24 wrapped sweets. These will look remarkably like jewels!

If you attach the sweets with small pieces of double sided sticky tape, one can easily be removed and eaten on each of the twenty four days during advent.

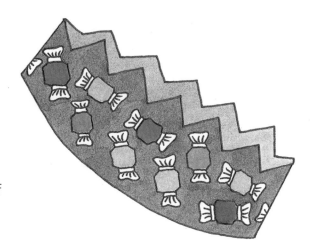

An Advent jigsaw calendar

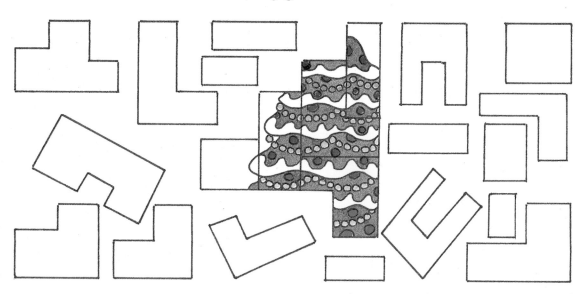

1 Create your Advent jigsaw by drawing and colouring a Christmassy scene on a sheet of card 20cm by 20cm. Alternatively, you could use a picture from a magazine pasted on to card.

2 Divide and cut the picture into 24 jigsaw pieces and lay the jigsaw face down.

3 Turn over a piece of the jigsaw each day during Advent until you have a complete picture on the twenty fourth day.

❧ A Father Christmas Advent calendar ☙

Count the days leading up to Christmas by making this attractive, surprise Advent calendar.

1 Simply draw a Father Christmas on his sleigh on a large sheet of thin card. Stick a strong paper bag on to the sleigh, making sure that you can open the top, of the bag.

2 Gather together 24 pieces of thin string or ribbon and attach a wrapped sweet or small surprise to the end of each one. Sellotape small cardboard disks to the strings and number the disks 1 to 24.

3 Pop the sweets into the bag, leaving the disks to hang down on the outside of the picture.

Each day the correct string can be removed and the surprise will be discovered.

Evergreen Decorations

The evergreen's ability to stay green and alive during the long winter months, when other plants seem to die, caused it to be seen as a magical plant. It became the symbol of everlasting life, fertility and the return of Spring.

Mistletoe

Mistletoe is also known as 'golden bough'. A parasitic plant, it grows as if by magic on the branches of different trees. It bears pure white berries in the season when other plants seem to be dead and because of this it has long been seen as a fertility symbol.

The ancient Scandinavians believed that if enemies met beneath mistletoe they would instantly become friends. The current custom of kissing beneath the mistletoe obviously has some connection with this belief as well as links with the fertility symbolism.

Holly and ivy

Holly was an easy plant to incorporate into the Christian church. The berries were said to represent Christ's blood and the prickles Christ's crown of thorns.

Ivy was more difficult for the Christians to accept because it had strong connections with Bacchus the Roman god of wine. However both holly and ivy have long been used as a means of decorating homes. Our ancestors believed that the plants would ensure the return of spring.

It is said to be unlucky to take evergreens down before the Twelfth Night. In the past however the boughs of greenery were often left in place until Candlemas, which is on February 2nd. Then they would be replaced with bunches of snowdrops, the snowdrop being an indication that the magic of the evergreen had worked and that the long awaited spring had arrived.

❧ Holly biscuits ❧

For the biscuits:

225g self raising flour
2 teaspoons cinnamon
pinch of salt
150g butter
100g caster sugar
1 beaten egg

For the decoration:

225g icing sugar
green food colouring
marzipan
red food colouring

1 Put the flour, salt and cinnamon into a bowl. Rub in the butter.

2 Add the sugar and then the beaten egg. Knead the mixture until you have a dough.

3 Wrap the dough in clingfilm and allow it to rest in the fridge for half an hour.

4 Roll out the dough until it is about 6mm thick.

5 Cut out some hollyshaped leaves from the dough. You can buy holly-shaped cutters or use a sharp knife.

6 Put the leaves on a greased baking tray and bake for 15 minutes in an oven set at 180C or gas mark 4.

When the cooked biscuits have cooled, you can decorate them.

1 Mix the icing sugar with a little water and the green food colouring. Spread a little of the green paste on top of each biscuit.

2 Add some red food colouring to the marzipan and use the mixture to make small red berries.

3 Put two or three red berries at the base of each leaf.

4 When the green icing has dried, sprinkle the leaves with a light dusting of icing sugar snow.

 Victorian greenery garlands

This green paper garland is simple to make.

1 Fold a large sheet of green paper in half three times, short edge to short edge. Draw a circle in the centre of the folded paper and cut out eight separate circles.

2 Using the illustration as a guide, fold each circle into quarters and then cut out a curved petal-shaped edge. Make curved cuts on alternate sides of each folded circle.

3 Gently unfold the circles and then glue them together petal to petal, by spreading a little glue around the outside edges. Add a little glue in the centre of each circle.

4 When dry, carefully pull the outside circles apart in order to extend the garland.

A Christmas wreath

1 In order to make this traditional 'welcome' wreath, take a bundle of long straw and bind it with raffia to form a sausage shape. Pull the two ends of the sausage together in order to create a circle and tie securely.

2 Take small bunches of evergreens and bind them to the circle with green garden string.

3 Tie a big red bow of ribbon around the top of the circle. Fruit, silver or gold sprayed fircones and smaller bows can also be attached to the circle by attaching them to florists wire and then pushing the pointed ends of the wire into the wreath.

A holly leaf necklace

1 Cut several holly leaves from a piece of green felt, making sure that each one has a 'stem'.

2 Glue the leaves on to a necklace string by folding the stems around the string. This necklace looks particularly pretty if you alternate the leaves with red wooden beads.

3 If you can't obtain red beads you could always cut out a piece of newspaper about 15cm by 15cm, roll it loosely around a pencil and stick it together with glue. When the glue has dried slide the pencil out leaving a hollow paper tube. Cut the tube into 1cm beads The beads can now be painted bright red.

Christmas roses

Use these roses mixed with real holly and ivy leaves to create
a wonderfully colourful table decoration.

1 Cut out 18 squares of red tissue paper,
six large (10cm by 10cm), six medium
sized (8cm by 8cm) and six small (6cm by
6cm).

2 Fold each square into four and, using the
illustration as a guide, draw a petal shape
on the folded paper. Cut round this
shape. Unfold all the papers.

3 Place a small petal shape on top of a
medium sized shape and finally place
both of these on top of a large petal
shape. Hold all three petals together by
pushing the tip of a green pipecleaner
through the centre of the flower then coil
it round to stop the petals falling off.
Gently curl and fold the petals into a
rose-like shape.

Christmas Cards

Until 1846 there was no such thing as a mass-produced Christmas card. Before this date calling cards, sometimes embellished with small pictures and verse, and used throughout the year by the upper classes, might have had a special message added at Christmas time, but the manufacture and sale of Christmas cards was unknown.

In 1846 Henry Cole, the first director of the Victoria and Albert Museum and a prominent member of the Royal Society of Arts, decided that he was too busy to write out his usual Christmas letters and asked the artist John Calcott Horsley to create a card with a festive design on the front which he could then sign and send to his friends and relatives. Being a businessman, Henry Cole also had some extra cards produced which he proceeded to sell for 1/- (5p) each.

By 1860 it had become a very common custom to send Christmas card greetings. In 1870 the half penny post for unsealed envelopes was introduced and the habit of sending cards became even more popular.

The design of Henry Cole's first card, showing a central rustic trellis work panel containing a happy family and two side panels containing pictures of poor people being clothed and fed, set the scene for the first cards. They often included the visual message of charity for the poor and needy.

By the time the cards had became cheaper and mass produced they resembled Valentine cards with lots of cherubs, lace and garlands of flowers. Gradually they became distinctively Christmas cards, with their own specifically Christmas appeal. Robins, Father Christmas, snow scenes and holly started to appear on the front of the cards. The Victorian habit of saving the pictures in special albums resulted in the verse being placed inside the card and the familiar formula for our Christmas messages was established.

 A pretty presents card

Happy Christmas!

1. Fold a sheet of 30cm by 22cm paper two times in order to create a folded card.

2. From several different scraps of pretty cotton material, cut out some small box shapes, varying in size and shape.

   Create 'string' on the boxes by drawing lines on top of the material.

3. Stick the boxes in an overlapping pile on the front of the card. The larger boxes should be the first ones to be stuck down and the smaller ones placed on top.

4. If you have used a dark-coloured paper for your card you could write the words 'Merry Christmas' on the front with a gold or silver pen. Metallic ink pens are available in the shops.

❧ A snowman card ❧

Use black or dark blue card for this picture.

1 On the front of the card draw a very simple outline. Spread glue all over the snowman and cover him with small cotton wool snowballs.

2 Cut out six circles from a small piece of black paper and stick these into position on the snowman, using three as buttons, two for his eyes and one for his nose.

3 Using some scraps of material cut out a hat and scarf and glue these into position on the snowman.

❧ A thumb-print reindeer card ❧

These happy-looking reindeer make a very attractive Christmas card.

1 Mix up some brown paint. Dip your thumb in the paint and create a thumb-print head and body for each reindeer. You might find that the prints look better if you first take off the excess paint by printing your thumb on a scrap of paper.

2 When the prints have dried, add all the fine details to the reindeer with a black felt-tip pen. And don't forget to give one of them a red nose!

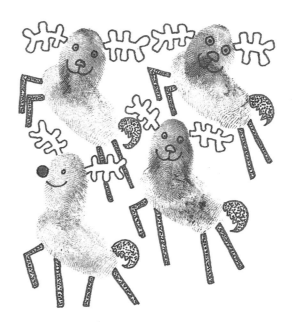

✿ Holly cards ✿

Here is a quick but effective way of producing Christmas cards.

1 Place some folded card on sheets of newspaper. (Green card looks particularly attractive.)

2 Lay several holly leaves on the front of each card and gently spray over the top of the leaves with metalic silver or gold spray paint.

3 Remove the leaves and add some red berries to the cards. The berries can be made from small circles of red felt or shiny red paper glued into position.

✿ A walking robin card ✿

1 On the front of each card draw the large outline shape of a robin, but don't add the robin's legs. Colour the robin and, if you like, add some background to the picture.

2 In the position where the robin's legs should be, cut out two circular holes just large enough for two fingers to push through. Children love to turn their fingers into the robin's legs.

 A stained-glass nativity card

1 Draw an arched window frame on the front of a sheet of card and cut it out with scissors. Using the cut out window as a template, draw the window on a sheet of thin white paper.

2 Create a Christmas picture inside the window on the white paper and colour it in using felt-tip pens. Cut the Christmas picture out but be sure to leave a border all the way round the outside. Use a small piece of cotton wool to rub a little cooking oil all over the reverse of the Christmas picture.

3 Stick the coloured picture into position behind the cut out card frame. Add a loop of ribbon to the top of the card so that it can be hung in a window where the daylight will shine through the nativity scene.

Christmas Stockings and Wrapping Paper

Stockings

There is a story which suggests that Saint Nicholas is responsible for the tradition of putting out stockings on Christmas Eve.

Apparently-long ago there was a nobleman who fell upon hard times. He had little money left and several daughters. The girls had hoped to marry the sons of a local Lord but the lack of money meant that they could have no dowry.

On Christmas Eve the weeping girls went to bed early, leaving their stockings hanging over the end of their bed. Saint Nicholas, taking pity on the girls, tossed some gold through their open window and the coins landed inside the stockings.

In the morning the delighted girls found the gifts lying in each of their stockings. With the money they were able to marry the young men of their choice and they lived happily ever after.

Wrapping paper

In Victorian times coloured paper was incredibly expensive and so most presents were wrapped in brown paper.

There were printed sheets of pictures and decorative letters, mostly produced in Germany, and these were sometimes cut out and used to decorate parcels. The Victorians would also use sequins, ribbons and frills of coloured paper to embellish parcels and in this way they created very personalised wrappings for their presents.

A cone-shaped container or cornucopia was a very popular Victorian package. These would be filled with sweets, nuts or raisins and hung on the Christmas tree.

The cornucopias were made at home from triangles of card, backed with coloured paper and formed into a cone shape. The cones were then decorated with cut-out pictures, ribbons and glittery borders.

❧ A teddy bear stocking ❧

This stocking makes an ideal container for a small Christmas gift.

You will need:

a piece of brown felt 40cm by 30cm
a piece of red felt 26cm by 30cm
a small piece of black felt
a small piece of white felt
strong glue
scissors
a black felt-tip pen

Using the illustration as a guide:

1 Cut out a stocking shape with a teddy bear's head on top from the brown felt.

2 Use the red felt to cut out a second identical stocking shape, minus head.

3 Stick the red felt stocking on top of the brown felt stocking. Make sure that you leave the head sticking out of the top and that you only glue around the outside edge of the stocking. Leave the top rim of the stocking free from glue.

4 Cut out two brown paws from the left over scraps of felt and stick them on to the top of the red stocking.

5 Cut out a nose and eyes from the black and white felt and stick them on to the teddy bear's head.

6 Fine details such as whiskers can be drawn on to the felt with the black felt-tip pen.

❧ A garland of Christmas stockings ❧

1 Take some thick paper and draw and cut
   out as many different stocking shapes as
   possible. Each stocking needs to be
   about 20cm long. It might be easier if
   you make a card template of a stocking
   shape and draw round this.

2 Decorate the stockings. Paint some, cover
   some with glitter pictures, and cut out
   pictures of toys from old catalogues to
   stick on to the rest.

3 Decide where you want to hang the
   stockings. Put some string or ribbon in
   position and fasten the stockings to it
   with paper clips.

❧ Holly leaf wrapping paper ❧

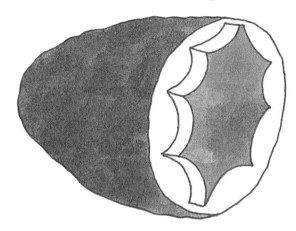

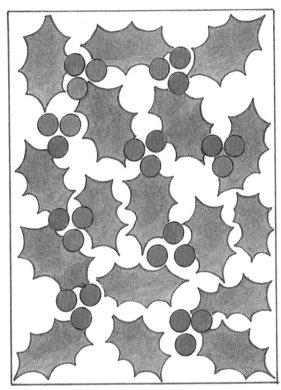

This is a quick and easy way to produce wrapping paper.

Take a potato and slice it in half. Cut out a holly leaf shape from one half of the potato, dip the holly shape in green paint and print holly leaves all over a roll of inexpensive lining paper. When the green paint has dried, dip your finger tips in red paint and add some red berries to the paper.

❧ Candle light wrapping paper ❧

1 Take a white candle and, using it rather like a crayon, draw some candle shapes all over a large sheet of white paper. To create the candle flames use yellow, red and orange wax crayons.

2 Mix up some dark blue water colour paint. Be sure to make it as thin and runny as possible.

3 Using a thick brush, gently wash the paint all over the sheet of paper. Of course the wax-treated paper will not absorb the paint and the candle shapes and flames will shine through.

❧ Speckled robin wrapping paper ❧

1 Cut out some robin-shaped stencils from a sheet of card and place the stencils on a sheet of coloured paper.

2 Dip an old toothbrush in some paint and rub your thumb along it so that the paint spatters over the robin stencils. Carefully lift the stencils and repeat the process.

To create a really pretty effect use two colours.

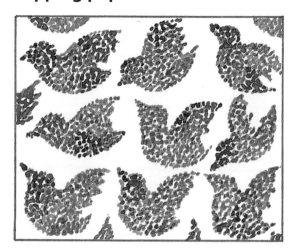

❧ Frosty hands wrapping paper ❧

Children love hand printing and this activity gives them the opportunity to produce some really pretty wrapping paper at the same time.

1 Mix some white water colour paint and carefully dip hands in the paint and then print them all over a sheet of coloured paper.

2 When all the hand prints have dried a frosty effect can be produced by dabbing spots of glue all over the hands and then sprinkling them with glitter.

Christmas Eve

Yule Logs

The custom of dragging home a large log on Christmas Eve and keeping it burning throughout the Christmas period comes to us from the ancient festival of Yule. This was a pagan festival celebrated by the Norse people in honour of their god Thor.

Traditionally the log was lit from kindling left over from the previous year's log and the new fire kept alive continually throughout the festival. In this way the people believed they benefited from the magical qualities of perpetual fire and so long as the flames were kept alive in the hearth they symbolised the undying sun. If the fire was allowed to go out it was thought to be extremely unlucky.

Fire and its association with the sun was particularly significant to the ancient people celebrating the winter solstice on December 21st. For this was the time when the sun was furthest from the equator and the dark cold winter must have seemed never ending.

The church tried to give the custom Christian significance by insisting the log should be from an ash tree. It is said the baby Jesus was first warmed by an ash fire , one of the few woods that will burn straight from the tree and used by the shepherds on the hillsides of Bethlehem.

It was also said to be unlucky to throw ashes out on Christmas day as it would be throwing them in the face of Christ. Finally, the ashes from the Christmas fire were said to be magical and thought to provide a cure for all manner of ailments, including toothache, as well as giving the ground on which they were thrown extra fertility.

Few homes these days have a hearth large enough for a giant sized Yule log but many homes still keep a fire burning continually throughout the Christmas period and most families have a chocolate log to eat.

🍃 A Yule log gift box 🍃

This is an especially easy way to wrap awkwardly shaped presents such as bottles.

1 Firstly, wrap the present in layers of tissue paper and then sellotape a layer of corrugated paper around the outside, making the present as log-shaped as possible.

2 Surround the corrugated paper with a layer of brown crepe paper and sellotape this into position.

3 On top of the 'log' stick some cotton wool snow and finally add some holly leaves as well as the present label.

🍃 A candle Yule log 🍃

This decoration makes an effective centre piece for the Christmas dinner table.

1 Drill a hole in the top of half a split log. (The hole needs to be big enough for a candle.)

2 Whip up some white soap powder and water until you have a thick paste and apply this to the top of the log to look like snow.

3 Place the candle in the hole and when the paste has dried, put the log on the table and arrange holly and ivy stems over and around it.

✍ A sherry log ✍

This pudding is extremely simple to make and yet it has a very special taste.

1 Take a packet of chocolate chip cookies and dip each one very quickly in a saucer of sherry.

2 Create a long log shape with the biscuits by sticking them together with whipped cream. Cover the outside of the log with more whipped cream.

3 Leave the log in the refrigerator for a couple of hours to allow the biscuits time to soak in the sherry.

4 Before serving, sprinkle the log with grated chocolate. Place a plastic robin on top and arrange a few holly leaves around the outside.

✍ A robin Yule log ✍

1 Take a piece of chicken wire and form a log shape. Cover the log with strip after strip of newspaper, soaking each strip with wallpaper paste as you do so.

2 Roll up a small ball of paper and cover it with strips of paste-covered paper.

3 Leave both the log and the ball to dry thoroughly.

4 When dry, paint the log with brown paint and paint the ball to look like a robin. The robin's wings and tail can be created by cutting out two half circles and a triangle from brown felt and sticking them on the body. Stick cotton wool snow on the log and add the robin.

You could also arrange some holly dipped in glue and glitter, or some silver sprayed fir cones around the log.

The Crib

A limestone cave near Bethlehem was the birth place of the baby Jesus. The caves were used for sheltering animals and the baby Jesus may well have been laid in a manger.

The Romans, wishing to desecrate the Christian shrine, actually turned the cave into a grotto dedicated to their god Adonis but later the Christian emperor Constantine ordered a magnificent church to be built over the cave. A church still stands on the site and it is known as St Mary of the Nativity.

The first Christmas Crib is said to have been created on Christmas Eve in 1223. It was made by St Francis of Assisi and was complete with live animals. Since this time the Christmas Crib has been a popular addition to the Christmas ritual.

Farmers in the mountains of central Europe would spend the long winter evenings carving marvellous figures for the nativity scene. In Italy, Germany, Austria and South America special classes are held where children can learn to create and build cribs in many different styles.

Most Christian churches, and sometimes village or town squares, now have a Christmas crib. It is a potent visual reminder of the nativity. There is also a traditional belief that the hay used in the manger of the Christmas Crib has special magical qualities and if it is fed to sick beasts it restores them to health.

❄ The baby in the manger finger puppet ❄

1 Take a small empty matchbox and cover the outside sleeve with pretty Christmas wrapping paper.

2 Remove the inner tray and, using the illustration as a guide, cut a slot in the sleeve and a hole in the bottom of the tray. Replace the tray.

3 On your finger nail draw a baby's face and wrap some cotton wool around the finger and secure with a rubber band.

4 Push the baby finger through the hole in the bottom of the box and open the matchbox to reveal the baby in the manger.

❧ A Christmas angel ❧

1 Wrap some tinfoil tightly around a toilet roll tube and sellotape it into position. Tuck the loose ends of the tinfoil into the top and bottom of the tube.

2 Glue a small paper doily into position behind the tube or, if you find the doily is too big, you could cut it in half.

3 Draw a circle on a sheet of white paper, cut it out, and draw a pretty angel's face on the circle. Glue the face on to the front of the tube.

A group of these angels suspended by thread makes a very attractive Christmas mobile.

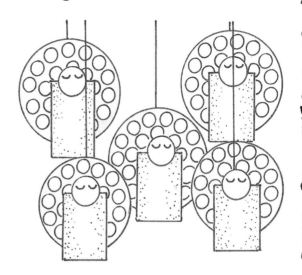

❧ A shoe box nativity scene ❧

1 To create a stable, cover the bottom of the shoe box with pretty Christmas wrapping paper and inside, paint or draw a stable scene.

2 Stand the shoebox on its side and cover the floor with cotton wool or straw. A sloping roof can be simply made from a piece of corrugated cardboard sellotaped into position.

3 To create the nativity scene, cut out the characters from last year's Christmas cards and stand them in small balls of plasticine. If you prefer, you could draw and cut out the characters from card.

❦ A Christmas star ❦

1 Cut out a star from a sheet of thick card and make a small hole near the tip of one of the points.

2 Glue a variety of pasta shapes on the front and back of the star and when they have dried, spray the star with metallic paint.

3 Thread a length of ribbon through the hole and hang the star in position.

Small stars created in this way are ideal for the Christmas tree, while large stars can be hung from the ceiling in groups to make pretty Christmas mobiles.

❦ A modelling dough crib ❦

1 Mix together 2 cups of salt and 4 cups of plain flour. Add some water to this mixture until you have formed a dough.

2 On a floury surface make the dough into two dimensional nativity models and fire them on a baking sheet in a very low oven for several hours. Remove the models when they are completely dry and hard.

3 When the models are cold, paint them with poster paint, and if you wish the colours to shine you could finish the models with a coat of varnish.

4 When the models are dry they can be arranged and stuck on to a suitably painted stable backdrop. (This can be simply made from a sheet of corrugated cardboard lined with white paper.)

The Christmas Tree

Long ago in the 8th Century there was an English monk called St Boniface who travelled to Germany in order to convert the people of that land to the Christian faith. During his visit he came across a group of pagans worshipping an oak tree and preparing to sacrifice a small child under the tree's great branches.

St Boniface was enraged. He lifted the child to safety and then, taking an axe, he cut down the mighty oak. Not surprisingly the heathens were enraged by what he had done and they were just about to take their revenge when St Boniface noticed a tiny little fir tree growing between the severed roots of the oak. He offered the pagans the tree as a symbol of the new faith and the small fir became a part of the Christian tradition.

This may be just a legend - or the story of St Boniface and the fir tree may contain a grain of truth. What is certain is that the first Christmas trees were found in Germany.

In Medieval Germany the people often watched 'Mystery' plays. The plays told simple Christian stories and were performed either in the large churches or in the open squares in front of the church. One particular play was very popular. It was called the 'Paradise' play, and basically it told the story of Adam and Eve. Of course Adam and Eve were banished from the Garden of Eden, but in the final act the audience were consoled by the promise of a coming saviour and the last scene depicted the birth of Christ in Bethlehem.

During performances of this play, a large fir tree surrounded by candles was often erected on the stage to represent both the 'Tree of life' and the 'Tree of discernment of good and evil'. Later, small 'Paradise' trees were taken into the homes of the faithful during the Christmas celebrations and in this way the first Christmas trees were established.

By the 15th Century the custom of erecting and decorating a small tree inside the home was becoming more and more popular in many parts of Germany. Traditions grew up about the way in which the tree should be decorated, and the decorations would include apples, to recall the fruit which tempted Adam, and small white bread wafers, representing the Holy Eucharist. In this way the decoration of the tree became associated with religious symbolism - the fruit of sin and the saving fruit of the sacrament. Later the wafers were made more elaborate and white dough was cut and baked in the shape of stars, angels, hearts, flowers and bells, while brown dough was used to create men, birds, dogs and other animals.

In earlier Medieval homes Christmas candles had been placed on a wooden pyramid-shaped structure. It now became the custom for the candles to be placed on the Christmas tree. There is also a story that Martin Luther, while out walking one starry Christmas Eve, was so impressed by the beauty of the stars that when he returned home he placed candles on the branches of a fir tree in order to remind children of the heavens from which the Christ child descended.

The symbol of the Christmas tree gradually spread and by the 19th Century it was to be found throughout Germany. In 1930 German immigrants took the tree to America. It had spread to France by 1837 when Princess Helen of Mecklenbury married the Duke of Orleans.

In England the Christmas tree arrived in the 1820's. It is often thought that Prince Albert introduced the first Christmas tree into England but in fact the German Princess Lieven had a tree decorated for the children of the English Court while she was on a visit to this country. It was several years later, in 1841, that Prince Albert had his tree set up in Windsor Castle. The Royal approval was enough to ensure that the tree rapidly gained in popularity both here and in America.

In many countries evergreens have always been a symbol of enduring life, and have long been a part of the traditional mid-winter celebrations. Before the arrival of the Christmas tree, it had been a custom in England to decorate the home with a 'Kissing Bough'. This was a spherical globe made from willow and covered with evergreens, red apples and candles, usually with a bunch of mistletoe in the centre.

The gifts which formerly had hung suspended from ribbons from the 'Kissing Bough' were now placed beneath the Christmas tree.

❧ A kissing bough ❧

Traditionally the base for this bough would be made from willow branches but a very good modern substitute can be created from two wire coathangers.

1 Pull the coat hangers into a circular shape and slide one inside the other to create a ball. Bind the top and bottom of the ball firmly together with strips of green garden twine .

2 With more twine bind bunches of evergreens on to the wire hoops until the entire ball is covered in green. At this point you may like to add a few baubles or small red apples. (For details of apple making see page 46).

3 From the centre of the bough hang a piece of fresh mistletoe. This can be attached with more twine..

Hanging the bough couldn't be simpler as the coat hanger handles at the top of the ball make very convenient hooks.

A Christmas tree for the wild birds

Bread trees   Cut out some tree shapes from slices of bread. Make a hole in the top of each one and then bake them in a cool oven until they are crisp.

Peanut garlands   Thread some peanuts on to string.

Peanut butter surprise   Spread fir cones with peanut butter.

Festive apples   Press sunflower seeds into an apple.

Coconut bells   Cut a coconut in half and make a hole in the shell with a corkscrew.

Millet pyramids   Tie three pieces of millet together to form a triangle.

❧ A fir cone Christmas tree ❧

1 Find a large 'open' fir cone and paint the tips of the cone with gold or silver enamel paint.

2 Paint an empty cotton reel with red enamel paint.

3 When the fir cone and the cotton reel are dry, you can glue the base of the cone 'tree' on to the top of the reel 'tub'.

4 When the glue has dried, decorate the tree by sticking tiny sequin baubles on to its branches.

An alternative Christmas tree

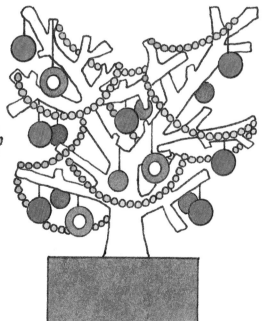

Take a winter walk through some local woodland and find a suitably sized fallen branch. The exact size rather depends on where you intend to put it in the house. The branch should be as full of twigs as possible.

On your return home, allow the branch to dry out and then paint it with white emulsion paint. When the branch has dried, stand it in a pot of earth and decorate it.

Christmas Tree Decorations

Charles Dickens gives a graphic account of the impact made on him by a Christmas Tree scene in 1850. ('A Christmas Tree' in Household Words 1850.)

"I have been looking on, this evening, at a merry company of children assembled round that pretty German toy, a Christmas tree. The tree was planted in the middle of a great round table, and towered high above their heads. It was brilliantly lit by a multitude of little tapers; and everywhere sparkled and glittered with bright objects. There were rosy-cheeked dolls, hiding behind green leaves; and there were real watches (with moveable hands, at least, and an endless capacity of being wound up) dangling from innumerable twigs; there were French-polished tables, chairs, eight-day clocks, and various other articles of domestic furniture (wonderfully made, in tin, at Wolverhampton), perched among the boughs, as if in preparation for some fairy housekeeping; there were jolly, broad-faced little men, much more agreeable in appearance than many real men – and no wonder, for their heads took off, and showed them to be full of sugar plums; there were fiddles and drums; there were tambourines, books, work-boxes, paint-boxes, sweetmeatboxes, peep-show boxes, and all kinds of boxes; there were trinkets for the elder girls, far brighter than any grown up gold and jewels; there were baskets and pin cushions in all devices; there were guns, swords and banners; there were witches standing in enchanted rings of pasteboard, to tell fortunes; there were tetotums, humming tops, needle cases, pen wipers, smelling-bottles, conversation-cards, bouquet-holders; real fruit, made artificially dazzling with gold leaf; imitation apples, pears, and walnuts, crammed with surprises; in short, as a pretty child, before me, delightfully whispered to another pretty child, her bosom friend, 'There was everything, and more.'"

❧ A Christmas dove ❧

1 Draw a simple bird shape on to a 20cm by 20cm sheet of white card and cut it out.

2 Using glue and silver glitter make an eye on both sides of the dove and stick some glitter on the beak.

3 With scissors make a 3cm slit through the middle of the dove.

4 Fold a sheet of 20cm by 20cm white paper as you would a fan and slot this through the slit in the dove. Gently pull the folded paper open so that it looks like the dove's wings.

5 Attach a loop of silver thread to the back of the dove and hang it on the tree.

✿ Bells, chimes and rings ✿

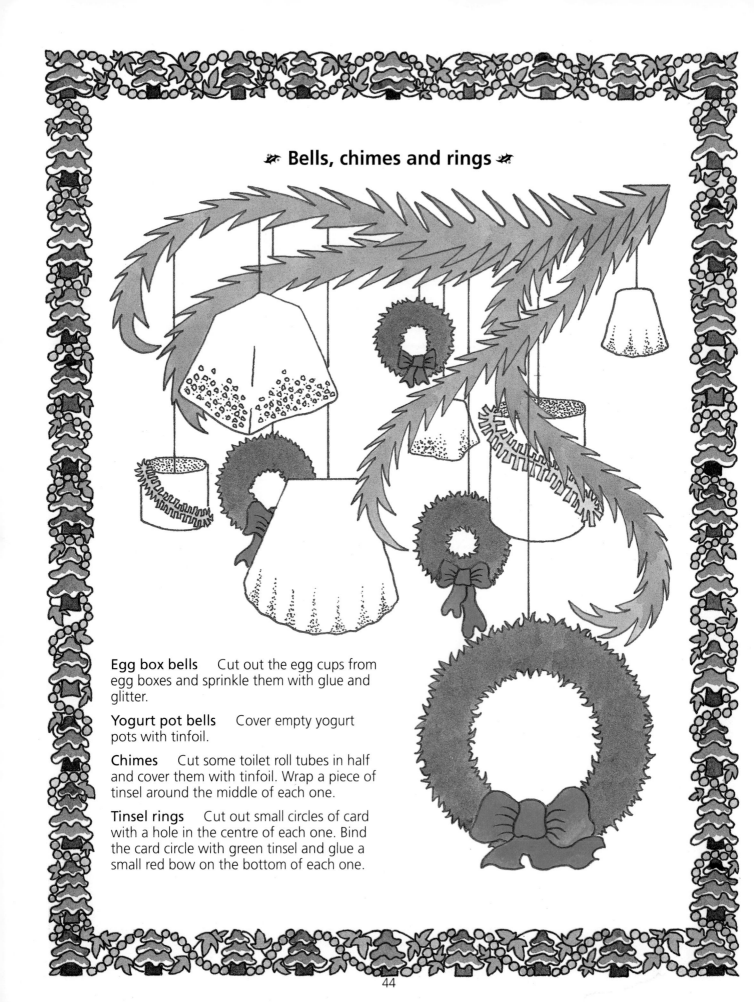

Egg box bells   Cut out the egg cups from egg boxes and sprinkle them with glue and glitter.

Yogurt pot bells   Cover empty yogurt pots with tinfoil.

Chimes   Cut some toilet roll tubes in half and cover them with tinfoil. Wrap a piece of tinsel around the middle of each one.

Tinsel rings   Cut out small circles of card with a hole in the centre of each one. Bind the card circle with green tinsel and glue a small red bow on the bottom of each one.

❧ A Christmas fairy ❧

No Christmas tree is quite complete without a fairy on the top.

1 The fairy's body and head is created by drawing a face on the top of a wooden clothes peg.

2 Her dress is made from pink tissue paper folded and glued into position.

3 Her hair is made from tiny pieces of yellow wool.

4 Her wings are made from two silver painted pipe cleaners twisted into two circles and glued side by side on to a sheet of white tissue paper. When dry, the tissue around the outside of the pipe cleaners is cut away leaving a very delicate pair of wings to be stuck on to the back of the fairy..

❧ Biscuit shapes ❧

1 Sift 50g of plain flour into a bowl and rub in 25g of butter or block margarine. Stir in 25g of caster sugar and sufficient beaten egg to form a stiff dough.

2 Roll out the dough on a floured surface and cut out diamond, star or animal shapes with any suitable cutters you have available. Make a small hole in the top of each shape.

3 Place the biscuits on a baking sheet and cook for 15 minutes in a moderate oven.

4 When they are cool, decorate the biscuits with coloured icing, jelly sweets, silver balls, sugar flowers, or hundreds and thousands.

5 When set, attach a loop of ribbon through the hole in each shape and hang them on the tree.

Christmas apples

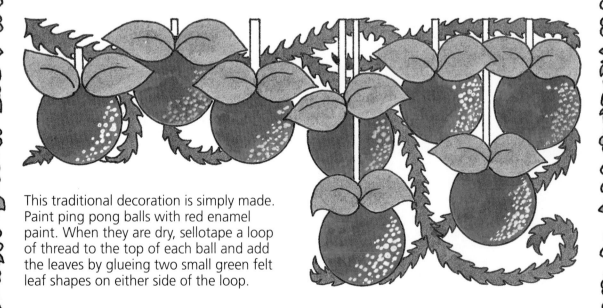

This traditional decoration is simply made. Paint ping pong balls with red enamel paint. When they are dry, sellotape a loop of thread to the top of each ball and add the leaves by glueing two small green felt leaf shapes on either side of the loop.

The Christmas Candle

Since medieval times a burning candle has been thought to represent both Christ and the star of Bethlehem. In England and France three candles are often used to symbolise the holy trinity.

Traditionally, candles would be placed in the centre of a laurel wreath and lit on the eve of the Christmas celebrations and kept burning during every night of the holy festival. If candles went out it was thought to bring extreme bad luck upon the household.

Each country seems to have its own method of displaying its candles. In Germany they are grouped on a wooden pyramid stand; in South America they are placed inside paper lanterns with Christmas symbols on the side; in Ireland the candle is wreathed with holly and placed in the window.

It seems likely that the widespread tradition of candle burning was adopted by the Christian church from the much earlier Jewish festival of Hanuca or the feast of lights. Certainly the two festivals are held at the same time of year.

Whatever the origins of the tradition, most countries have candles at Christmas time and they add a particular touch of magic to the festivities.

❧ A paper candle decoration ❧

1 Cover a toilet roll tube with tinfoil. Cut 1cm tabs round the base of the tube and bend them outwards. Glue the cut base of the tube to a circle of coloured card and stick a shiny red paper flame shape into the top of the tube.

2 Decorate the base of the candle with tinsel, small baubles or fir cones.

A paper lantern

These paper party lanterns look most attractive if you string dozens of them from the ceiling.

1 Fold a rectangular sheet of coloured paper in half lengthwise. Then with a pencil and ruler draw a line 2cm from the top along the cut, not the folded edge.

2 Mark the folded edge with a series of dots 1cm apart then, taking a pair of scissors, cut from each dot down to the pencil line. Make sure that you have cut through both thicknesses of paper.

3 Unfold the paper and curve round the short sides so that they meet. Sellotape the lantern into this final shape.

4 Make a loop from a separate length of coloured paper and attach it to the inside edge of the lantern.

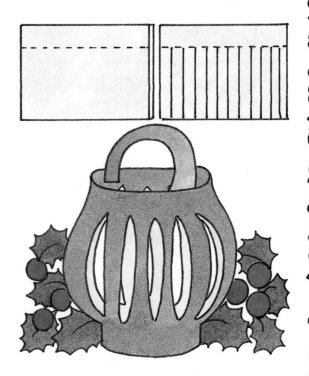

A candle window pane

This candle picture looks extremely pretty if stuck to a window pane.

1 Draw some simple candle and flame shapes on to a sheet of black paper. Try not to get too close to the edge of the paper and don't draw the shapes too close together. Cut the shapes out. This will leave lots of holes.

2 Lay the cut paper on to a covered table top and stick coloured tissue paper over the holes. When it is dry, you can hang the picture on a window where the light will shine through the tissue.

Ornamental lights

If you are giving a Christmas party, brighten up the dark garden path leading to your house by putting out some special Christmas candles.

Take a packet of tinfoil pudding basins and cut out some star shapes from both the tops and the sides. This is best done with a sharp Stanley knife.

Place night light candles on saucers and cover each candle with a pudding basin. When the candles are lit they shine very prettily through the star-shaped holes.

❧ Candle smoke pictures ❧

The presence of candles at Christmas time makes the creation of smoke pictures a most suitable activity.

1 Light a candle and hold a large white pottery plate just above the flame. Turn the plate slowly so that all of its surface gets covered with black soot.

2 Using your finger or a cocktail stick, draw Christmassy pictures in the soot.

3 When you have finished with one picture hold the plate above the flame and start again.

Please note: young children will need to be very carefully supervised when making these pictures.

Christmas Day

Saint Nicholas

The idea of the gods bringing gifts to the people in the winter time goes back to the beginnings of history. The Norsemen's god, Woden, was generous with gifts during his midwinter festival and there are many stories of him riding across the frozen land on his horse leaving presents for people. The Romans, during the festival of Saturnalia, also encouraged the giving of presents in honour of their god.

The people were fond of their midwinter gifts but the Christian church, not unnaturally, preferred to change the pagan gods to a Christian saint. They chose Saint Nicholas for the task.

It has become a tradition on December 6th, Saint Nicholas's Eve, especially on the continent, for children to put out their shoes and stockings which are filled by the generous saint with toys, sweets and gingerbread.

Father Christmas as we know him today, with his white beard and red clothes, although a direct decendent of Saint Nicholas, is a completely 19th century invention. Until then, Father Christmas or Saint Nick had been a rather vague figure and had varied between a tall bearded man with a holly wreath on his head to a hunchback with a three cornered hat and glasses.

The bright red colour for his costume was actually made popular by a 20th century advertisement for coca cola. Before the advertisement several colours had been used, including blue.

The term Santa Claus also became well known at this time. 'Sinter Klaass' is the Dutch for Saint Nicholas, and immigrants to the United States from Holland continued to use the term. It became anglicised, and the Americans adopted it with its new · spelling, creating a new name for the favourite saint of all children.

✍ Father Christmas's nose ✍

This is a quickly made toy which will be much appreciated if popped inside a Christmas stocking.

1 Draw and colour Father Christmas's profile, minus nose, on a sheet of card.

2 Make two small holes in the profile, one on each side of the gap where the nose should be.

3 Take the unwanted chain from a necklace and push each end of the chain through the holes in the card. The length of chain hanging down should be about double the width of the space for the nose.

4 Sellotape the chain into position on the underside of the card. The card can now be tilted and shaken to make the chain form many different Santa noses.

❧ A Santa gift box ❧

1 Roll some red crepe paper round a toilet roll tube and fasten it in position with a little piece of Sellotape. Tuck the loose ends of the paper inside the tube.

2 Cut out a black paper strip 1cm by 15cm and stick this round the middle of the tube. This will form Santa's belt.

3 Cut out a circle from pink paper, about the size of a 10p coin, and draw a happy face on it before sticking it into position on the tube.

4 Take some pieces of cotton wool and glue these round Santa's face to form hair and a beard.

5 Glue the completed Santa on to a cardboard disk and pop a chocolate bar or similar small gift into the top of the tube.

❧ A reindeer party hat ❧

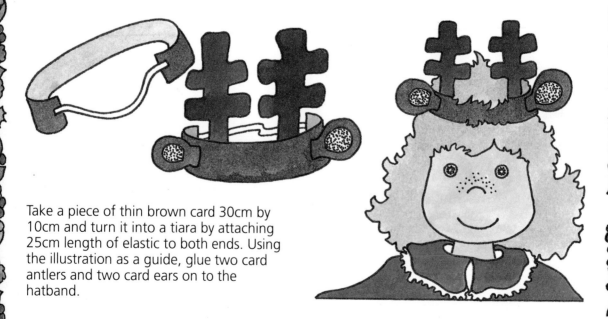

Take a piece of thin brown card 30cm by 10cm and turn it into a tiara by attaching 25cm length of elastic to both ends. Using the illustration as a guide, glue two card antlers and two card ears on to the hatband.

❧ A pop up Santa ❧

This surprise toy is very popular with little children.

1 Sellotape a piece of red paper to the outside of a toilet roll tube.

2 The tube can be turned into Santa's body (minus head) by the addition of two paper cut out arms and hands and finer details such as his buttons and belt can be drawn in position.

3 Draw Santa's face on a circle of card (the circle should be about the size of a 10p coin) and add his beard by glueing cotton wool on to the circle.

4 With a small piece of Sellotape attach the circle face to the top of a thick drinking straw.

5 Push the straw up through the tube until the face peeps out. Little children love to play 'Peep-O' with these figures.

❧ A Father Christmas snowstorm ❧

Children love glass jar snowstorms and this home-made version is particularly festive.

1 Mix up some waterproof filler and carefully spoon it into the bottom of a clean empty glass jar. The jar needs to have a screw-top lid.

2 While the filler is still wet stand a plastic Father Christmas, (the type which usually decorates the Christmas cake) into the bottom of the jar.

3 Allow the filler to dry completely.

4 When the filler has dried pour cold water into the jar and add some 'snow' glitter. Screw the lid back on the jar and shake!

Christmas Crackers

Crackers, or cosaques as they were formerly known, have only been around since Queen Victoria's reign. It was during that time that a former pastry baker by the name of Thomas Smith went on holiday to France and while in Paris spotted some interesting looking sweets or bonbons for sale. The bonbons were wrapped in colourful paper with a twist at each end.

Tom Smith brought the idea back to England with him and was soon producing minature surprise parcels which contained not only sweets but small gifts such as perfume and jewellery. The crackers also contained mottoes. Tom Smith was particularly proud of these mottoes, commissioning quite famous writers to pen the miniature works. An early example went as follows:

"The sweet crimson rose with its
   beautiful hue
Is not half so deep as my passion for you.

T'will wither and fade, and no more will
   be seen
But while my heart lives you will still be
   its queen."

But what gave the cracker its crack, was Tom Smith's later invention of two strips of card dipped in a chemical which make a small bang when they are pulled apart. It is said that Tom was sitting by the fire one night listening to the crackling fire when he wondered if he could produce a surprise crackle in his product. After much experimentation the bang was produced and the cracker lived up to its name.

Tom Smith's factory in Norwich is still producing millions of crackers for Christmas, although it is only fair to say that most modern versions do not have the same artistic extravagance outside, or the same quality of gifts inside.

❧ A decorated cracker ❧

Making your own home made crackers is simple to do. They don't of course have a snap to make a bang, but the present inside can be extra special and the decoration on the outside can be very much more exciting.

1 Simply take a sheet of crepe paper 18cm by 32cm and a sheet of thin paper 16cm by 30cm and lay the thin paper in the centre of the crepe paper.

2 Take two empty toilet roll tubes and cut one in half across the middle. Cover the tubes with a little glue and lay them in position on the paper as in the illustration. Inside the centre tube put a home-made motto or joke and a small gift. Roll the tubes in the paper until they are tightly wrapped up and glue or sellotape the paper into position.

3 Use a little ribbon to tie a bow in the spaces between the tubes. Decorate the cracker with glitter, cut-out shapes, sequins, or small bunches of sprayed fir cones and leaves.

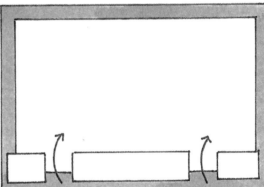

✱ A Christmas cracker party hat ✱

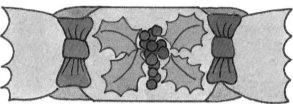

1 To make your hat, take a strip of card 60cm by 10cm and curl it into a hat shape. Sellotape the card into position.

2 Take a second sheet of coloured card 30cm by 10cm and cut out a cracker shape. Decorate the cracker with cut-out shiny paper shapes, e.g. stars.

3 Put a little glue on the front of the hat and press the cracker shape on to the glue. Only the centre of the cracker should be attached to the hat.

✱ Christmas cracker place cards ✱

1 For each place card you will need an empty matchbox, a sheet of thin paper 13cm by 8cm, a sheet of coloured card 20cm by 4cm, glue, scissors, Christmas wrapping paper and sugar-coated almonds or mints.

2 Cover the outside of each matchbox with the thin paper and glue this in position. Cut out some cracker shapes from the coloured card and glue them on to the front of each matchbox.

3 From the wrapping paper cut out some capital initial letters for each of your guests' names and glue these on to the front of the crackers.

4 Pop a few sweets inside each matchbox and stand the crackers on the table.

 A Pinata

In Mexico they have a special decorated container full of surprises which hangs from the ceiling at Christmas time. The children are blindfolded and allowed to hit the container or Pinata with sticks until it breaks and all the surprises are released.

Traditionally the container is made from pottery but you can make a Pinata from paper.

1 Blow up a balloon, cover it with Vaseline and then with layers and layers of paste-soaked strips of paper.

2 When the paper has completely dried, pop the balloon and pull it out.

3 Paint a Father Christmas face on the outside of the Pinata shape and glue on a cotton wool beard.

4 Pop a few unbreakable surprises inside the shape and attach ribbons to the top with some glue. Hang your Pinata in a suitable place and give the children a blindfold each and a roll of newspaper. When they are able to knock the Pinata to the ground they can take out the surprises.

The Christmas Feast and Table Decorations

Christmas seems almost inseparable from food. There is no traditional time for the main meal. It can be eaten at lunch time or in the evening but the menu is firmly established: turkey, pudding and mince pies.

Turkey

A reference to turkey as being one of the courses in a Christmas dinner dates back as far as the court of King Henry VIII.

Before turkey became so popular all manner of other birds would have been considered suitable Christmas fare. Goose and cockerel were popular with the less well off, while the rich would dine on peacock.

Christmas pudding or Plum pudding

This pudding was made even more popular by Prince Albert who is said to have been exceedingly fond of it. Traditionally the pudding was made on Stir Up Sunday, the last Sunday before Advent. Each person in the family would stir the pudding in an anti-clockwise direction and make a wish. Finally three charms were placed in the pudding, a ring to symbolise marriage, a thimble to symbolise a blessed life and a coin to symbolise wealth. The eventual finders of the charms would have these blessings bestowed upon them.

Mince pies

These were originally eaten at the beginning of the meal and used to contain minced meat. The meat was eventually replaced with suet and dried fruits and the pies were left until the end of the meal.

Before the Reformation the pies were oblong in order to symbolise the crib and often a small pastry baby was baked on the top. After the restoration of the monarchy in the 17th Century they became round with no baby on the top.

✿ Date, nut and rum mincemeat ✿

200g stoned dates
200g sultanas
200g raisins
100g dried apricots
200g chopped, peeled apple
150g chopped walnuts
100g mixed peel
200g suet
250g brown sugar
1 teaspoon cinnamon
1 teaspoon nutmeg
1 teaspoon ground cloves
grated rind and juice of 2 lemons
150ml dark rum

This very rich mincemeat will keep for many years.

1 Simply place all the ingredients in a bowl and mix well. If the mixture seems a little too dry, add more rum.

2 Cover the bowl with a clean tea towel and leave for two days.

3 Stir well again, spoon the mixture into clean jars, seal with jam pot covers and store in a cool place.

✿ Marshmallow mince pies ✿

125g of ready-made shortcrust pastry
mincemeat
12 pink and white marshmallows
3 glacé cherries cut into quarters

1 Roll out the pastry on a floured surface. Cut out twelve circles of pastry and use these to line a patty tin.

2 Spoon a little mincemeat into each pastry case and bake in a pre-heated oven, 200C or gas mark 6, for ten to fifteen minutes.

3 When the tarts are ready, remove them from the oven and place a marshmallow in the centre of each one. Return the tarts to the oven for one minute or just long enough to melt the marshmallow slightly.

4 Take the tarts out of the oven, carefully place a piece of cherry on top of each tart and cool them on a wire rack.

A 19th century plum pudding recipe

675g raisins
225g currants
335g breadcrumbs
225g flour
335g beef suet chopped finely
9 eggs well beaten
1 wineglass of brandy
225g mixed peel chopped
half a grated nutmeg
a pinch ground ginger

1 Mix together the raisins, currants, breadcrumbs, flour, suet, mixed peel, grated nutmeg and ginger.

2 Stir in the eggs and the brandy and mix thoroughly together.

3 Put the mixture into a buttered mould and steam for six hours.

❧ Christmas pudding truffles ❧

This recipe makes 16 delightful minature puddings, ideal for a
Christmas party or as a home made present.

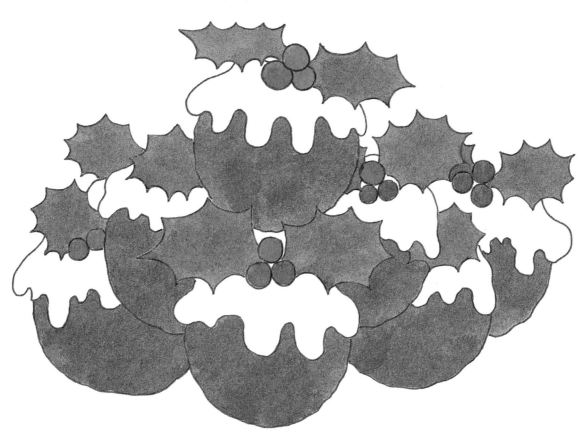

For the truffles:

50g butter
125g icing sugar
2 tablespoons cocoa
2 tablespoons of double cream
a few drop of vanilla essence
250g cake crumbs

To decorate:

chocolate sugar strands
50g icing sugar
16 minature plastic holly sprigs

1 Cream the butter and icing sugar
together. Gradually add the cocoa,
cream, vanilla essence and cake crumbs
to the mixture.

2 Roll the mixture into 26 small balls and
then roll the balls in the chocolate sugar
strands.

3 Mix 50g of icing sugar with a teaspoon
of hot water and then drop a small
amount of icing on to each truffle. Press
a holly sprig into the top a each
pudding.

✖ Victorian oranges and lemons ✖

The Victorians must have had a very sweet tooth. The oranges and lemons created by this recipe used to be arranged at Christmas time on branches of bay leaves and served with thick custard and chocolate biscuits.

To make the oranges and lemons:

285g Carolina Rice
30g arrowroot
the rind of a lemon cut thinly
115g sugar
two and a half pints of milk
10 drops of vanilla essence

1 Mix all the ingredients together and boil until firm. Spread the mixture out on a dish and when the dough is nearly cold, use floured hands to mould the dough into orange and lemon shapes.

2 Make a syrup by heating together 455g of sugar, the juice of three oranges and 15g gelatine dissolved in half a pint of water.

3 While the syrup is still hot divide it into two bowls and add a pinch of saffron to one of the bowls.

4 Finish the oranges by brushing them with the saffron syrup.

5 The lemons are finished by coating them with egg yolk and lemon juice and, when they are dry, brushing them with some of the syrup which does not contain saffron.

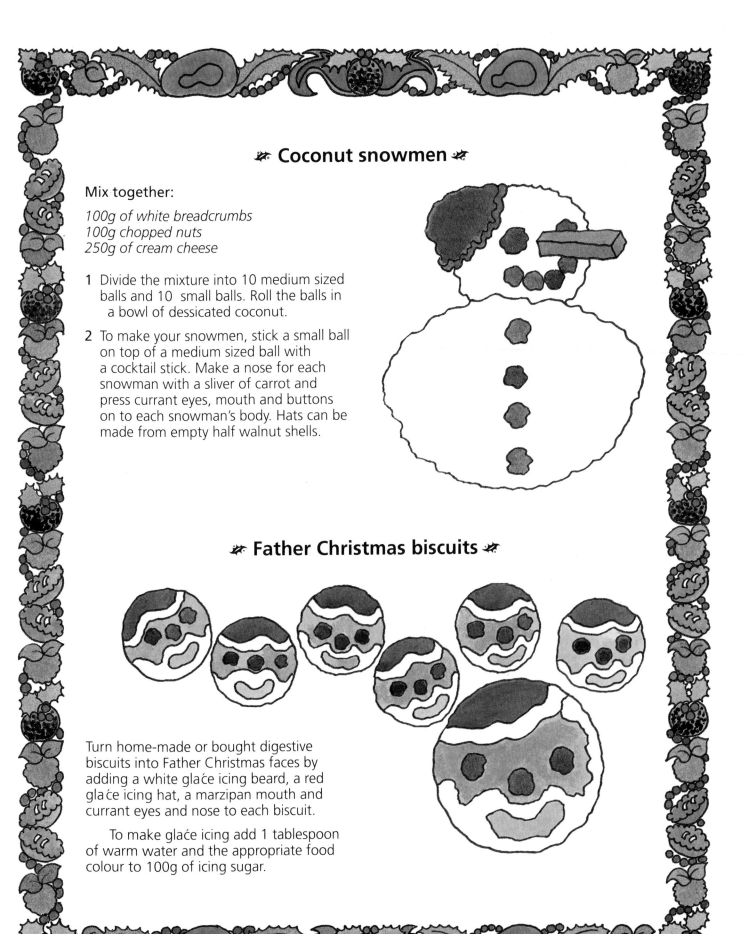

❧ Coconut snowmen ❧

Mix together:

100g of white breadcrumbs
100g chopped nuts
250g of cream cheese

1 Divide the mixture into 10 medium sized balls and 10 small balls. Roll the balls in a bowl of dessicated coconut.

2 To make your snowmen, stick a small ball on top of a medium sized ball with a cocktail stick. Make a nose for each snowman with a sliver of carrot and press currant eyes, mouth and buttons on to each snowman's body. Hats can be made from empty half walnut shells.

❧ Father Christmas biscuits ❧

Turn home-made or bought digestive biscuits into Father Christmas faces by adding a white glaće icing beard, a red glaće icing hat, a marzipan mouth and currant eyes and nose to each biscuit.

To make glaće icing add 1 tablespoon of warm water and the appropriate food colour to 100g of icing sugar.

🦌 A basket for home-made sweets 🦌

Using the illustration as a guide:

1 Take a square of thin card, 15cm by 15cm. Fold the card in half four times, so that when it is opened out you have 16 squares.

2 On each of the four corners, slit the corner squares to the first crease. These corner squares are then folded over and glued on to the two end centre squares. This forms a square, box-shaped basket.

3 Attach a strip of card across the centre of the box to create a handle.

The basket can be decorated in a variety of ways, with glitter or ribbon, or cut out Christmas motifs from last year's Christmas cards.

❧ White mice ❧

125g caster sugar
2 egg whites
24 split almonds
36 sweet silver balls
red liquorice laces cut into 10cm lengths
baking parchment

1 Whisk the egg whites until they are frothy and dry. Gradually whisk in the sugar.

2 Put the mixture into a piping bag with a wide nozzle and pipe the mixture on to a baking try lined with parchment paper. You should aim to pipe mouse shapes, with one end slighty rounded and the other end slightly pointed. A wet knife might help to adjust the shape.

3 Place the almonds in position at the pointed end to create ears and use the silver balls to form the eyes and nose.

4 Bake in a very cool oven 110C, gas mark quarter, for two hours.

5 Allow the cooked mice to cool on the parchment and then, using a cocktail stick, make a small hole in the tail end of each mouse. Stick a piece of liquorice in the hole to form a tail.

❧ A Christmas pudding gift box ❧

Here is a delicious container for a small Christmas gift.

Merry Christmas Nicholas James.

1 Blow up a balloon and smear the top half with Vaseline. Make up a jar of wallpaper paste and rip some newspaper into strips. Soak the newspaper strips in the paste and stick them over the greased balloon, making sure that you build up quite a thick layer of paper. Leave the paper-covered balloon in a warm place to dry out and harden.

2 When the paper is dry, remove the balloon and paint the pudding shaped box with appropriate Christmas pudding colours. Don't forget the cream!

3 When the paint has dried, stand the pudding on a paper plate and decorate it with holly. Small presents can be popped inside the pudding box.

❧ A snowman bonbon box ❧

Merry Christmas Kate Elisabeth

1 Using some glue and cotton wool, cover a toilet roll tube with pretend snow. Take a 5cm by 10cm piece of black paper and cut out six tiny circles. Stick these into position on the tube using two for the eyes, one for a nose and three as buttons. Cut out a small mouth from red paper and stick it on to the snowman.

2 Now to make his hat. Take a 10 cm by 10 cm piece of black paper, cut out a circle, slightly larger than the top of the snowman's body and rest it on top of snowman. Make a tube shape with a 2 cm by 10 cm piece of black paper and stick this on top of the black paper circle.

3 Put the snowman on a small white paper plate, lift off his hat and fill his body with sweets. Surround the snowman with cotton wool snow sprinkled with glitter and arrange small sprayed fir cones and holly in the snow.

❧ A decorated candle bottle ❧

1 Pour some emulsion paint (preferably red) inside a clear glass bottle. Put the cork back in the bottle and shake well. Pour out any left over liquid.

2 Cut out some shiny paper holly, ivy and berry shapes and glue them on to the outside of the bottle.

3 Stand a red candle in the bottle.

❧ Marshmallow snowmen place cards ❧

1 To make the snowman's body and arms, thread four white marshmallows on to a cocktail stick. Push a second cocktail stick through the middle of the marshmallows.

2 Decorate the snowman by wrapping a liquorice strip 'scarf' round his neck. Stick two Smartie eyes and a nose on to his face with a little glacé icing. (For glacé icing mix together 1 tablespoon of warm water with 100g of icing sugar).

3 Add the place cards by writing out and colouring a tiny Christmas card for each guest at the table. Hang a card on each snowman.

Boxing Day

Boxing Day and Christmas Pantomimes.

Alms boxes used to be hung in parish churches over the Christmas period for donations to the poor. The money collected was traditionally distributed on St Stephen's day, December 26th, which was therefore known as Boxing day.

Another link with the term 'Christmas Box' comes from the old custom of servants collecting money from their masters over the Christmas period in small earthenware boxes. The boxes were broken open on Boxing day.

The tradition of giving 'Christmas Boxes' has continued to the present day in terms of giving money at Christmas time to those who help us throughout the year. These days a Christmas box is usually given to your milkman, postman etc before the festivities start.

Nowadays, perhaps the most traditional association for most people is that between Boxing day and the pantomime.

The modern pantomime follows a firmly established traditional format which was influenced very strong by the Victorian music hall. With a villain to hiss and boo, a horse made from two people, a principal boy who is really a girl and a dame who is really a man, the characters usually burst into song at every conceivable opportunity.

But this modern pantomime follows a tradition of mumming or miming on Boxing day which is very ancient in its origins. Pantomime means 'all in mime' and originally the plays were entirely mimed.

Often in the past an entire village would take part in the Boxing day mime and the masked actors would call at as many houses as possible for their reward of spiced ale. In those days the favourite characters were not based on fairy tales like Babes in the Wood or Aladdin, but St George and the dragon and Father Christmas and the Wicked Turk.

 A hobby horse

This hobby horse (or donkey) makes an ideal prop for a Christmas play or nativity.

1 Stuff a large sock with balls of newspaper.

2 Push a strong garden cane into the sock and tie the sock securely to the cane with string.

3 Draw and cut out two large cardboard eyes and ears and glue these on to the hobby horse. You can also glue on a wool mane and a ribbon bridle.

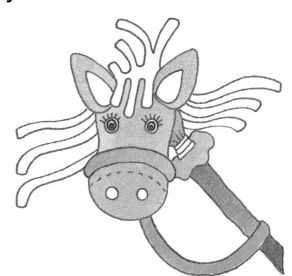

Pantomime masks

You don't need elaborate costumes for a Christmas pantomime. If the actors are wearing masks they can happily perform, with the minimum of costume.

There are two quick and simple ways of producing masks.

1 Take a large paper (never plastic) bag and draw and colour a face on to the front of the bag. Cut out two eye holes and put the bag over your head.

2 Take a large paper plate, draw a face on the front, cut out two eye holes and attach a loop of elasticated thread to the edge of the plate.

❦ A potato puppet show ❦

Children and adults adore puppet shows and these puppets are quickly and easily made.

1 Use a large washed potato for each puppet. Push a length of garden cane into a potato to create a head and body.

2 Draw and cut out eyes, nose and mouth from paper and attach these to the potato head with dressmaking pins. Use more pins to put wool hair on the head, and attach a length of fabric to the underpart of the potato.

3 The fabric can be wrapped around the cane in order to create a body.

A paper plate puppet show

1 Using the illustration as a guide, cut out some arms and legs from a very large sheet of cardboard. If you cut up old grocery boxes you don't need to buy expensive cardboard.

2 Attach the arms and legs to a paper plate head and a paper plate body by using string and Sellotape as shown in the illustration.

3 The head can be decorated with wool or ribbon hair and coloured with felt-tip pens. The body could have material scraps stuck on to it.

If a length of elasticated thread is attached to the top of the puppet's head, it will bounce up and down and dance quite realistically.

New Year's Eve

New Year's Eve
or
Hogmanay

There are many traditions associated with New Year's Eve, varying slightly, depending on which part of the country you live in.

On New Year's Eve you should pay your debts, return anything borrowed, clean the house and wind up all the clocks.

All windows and doors are opened before midnight, pots and pans are banged very noisily to drive out the evil spirits and the windows and doors shut again as the clock strikes midnight.

The first person to enter the house after midnight is known as the first footer. The first footer brings with him good luck or bad luck. If he is a dark-haired (or red-haired in Scotland) person, carrying a piece of coal, salt, bread, a sprig of evergreen and a sprig of mistletoe you will receive good luck in terms of warmth, health and hospitality for the coming year.

If the person is a flat-footed, fair-haired, lame, cross-eyed, knife-carrying female, then you will have bad luck for the next year. If you do have such an unfortunate first footer, you can, it seems, rid yourself of the bad luck by throwing salt on the fire, speaking to her before she speaks to you and crossing yourself.

The first footer comes in at the front door and out through the back door to make sure their good luck passes all through the house.

Hogmanay

The people of Scotland were greatly upset by the crushing of Christmas by the Puritans and so they transferred their feasting and merry making to New Year's Eve or Hogmanay. This emphasis on Hogmanay rather than Christmas continued in Scotland even after the reinstatement of Christmas and to the Scots the real fun begins on New Years Eve.

A frosted window new year banner

This New Year Greeting is quick to make and looks very festive against a dark winter sky.

1 Put a cup of washing soda in a bowl. Add a cup of hot water and stir with a spoon until all the crystals disappear.

2 Dip a sponge or wide paint brush into the warm liquid and use it to write out your New Year message on the surface of a window.

3 After about twenty minutes the liquid dries leaving behind frost-like crystals. When the party is over the message can easily be removed with a damp cloth.

❧ Happy New Year cards ❧

These cards use up your old Christmas cards and wrapping paper to create a pretty reminder of Christmas as well as wishing the recipient a happy new year.

1 Take a sheet of coloured card approximately 40 cm by 20 cm and fold it in half.

2 On the front of the card draw and cut out a large bell shape and under the bell, print the words Happy New Year.

3 Inside the card create a colourful collage by cutting out lots of Christmas shapes, such as robins, holly, snowmen, reindeer etc. from old Christmas cards and wrapping paper and sticking the shapes on to the card. The shapes and pictures should overlap each other.

When the card is standing upright the collage can be seen through the bell shape.

A paper plate calendar

1 Take two paper plates and cut out the centre from one of them. Use this centre as a circle template. Place it on top of a colourful picture in a magazine and draw round the card circle. Cut the picture out and glue it in to the centre of the second paper plate.

2 Spread a little glue around the outside edge of the picture plate and sprinkle some glitter on to the glue.

3 Stick a calendar booklet on to the bottom edge of the plate and glue a loop of ribbon on to the back of the plate at the top.

❄ New Year punch ❄

1 Press five cloves into an orange and bake it in the oven for half an hour. (gas mark 4, 180 degrees C)

2 Slice the orange and put the pieces in a saucepan with 2 bottles of ginger beer and a piece of cinnamon stick. Heat the liquid but do not let it boil.

3 When the punch has cooled slightly, serve it in frosted glasses.

4 **To frost each glass** Use whipped egg white and a fine paint brush to paint the outside of the glasses with pictures of snowmen. Put some caster sugar on a tray and roll the glasses in the sugar. The sugar will stick to the egg white and the pictures will be seen. Dip the rim of each glass in egg white and then dip the rims in caster sugar. Leave the glasses to dry for a few hours before using them with your special punch.

🌿 Black bun 🌿

In Scotland this delicious cake is traditionally eaten on New Year's Eve. Ideally it should be made weeks before New Year.

To make the pastry:

200g plain flour
a pinch of salt
100g butter
egg yolk for the glaze

For the filling:

400g currants
400g raisins
50g candied peel
100g chopped blanched almonds
100g plain flour
100g soft brown sugar
1 teaspoon each of ground cinnamon, ginger, allspice, nutmeg
1 level teaspoon cream of tartar
1 level teaspoon bicarbonate of soda
1 whisked egg
8 tablespoon of whisky
3 level tablespoons of black treacle

1 Make the pastry.

2 Grease a 20 cm round cake tin.

3 Mix all the filling ingredients together. The treacle will need heating in a pan to make it runny before it is added.

4 Use two thirds of the pastry to line the cake tin, making sure that the pastry comes up above the sides of the tin. Spoon the filling into the lined tin.

5 Roll out the remaining pastry and make a top for the tin. Moisten the edges of the pastry before you put the top on. Press the edges firmly together. Use any left over bits of pastry to make some letters and write Happy New Year on top of the lid.

6 With a skewer make five or six holes right down to the bottom of the cake.

7 Glaze with egg yolk.

8 Bake in the centre of the oven, (gas mark 4, 180 degrees C) for two and a half hours. If the pastry appears to be getting too brown while cooking you can cover it with foil.

9 Turn out of the tin and allow to cool.

10 Store the cake in an airtight tin, wrapped in foil.

Twelfth Night

The Epiphany

January 6th is known as the Twelfth Night or Epiphany. The word Epiphany means 'showing' and refers to the showing of the baby Jesus to the three wise men.

Epiphany also marks the end of the Christmas celebrations and is the date when all the Christmas decoration should be pulled down. It is thought to bring twelve months of bad luck if the tree and the evergreens and cards are not removed on this day.

In fact Twelfth Night has not always been the day that marked the end of Christmas. In the past the celebrations went on until the feast of Candlemas on February 2nd.

These days, apart from pulling the decorations down, the majority of families do not mark the day in any special way. However , in the past it was the day for a final celebration. A Twelfth Night cake would have been baked containing a pea and a bean. The finders of the pea and bean became the King and Queen of the party and the rest of the gathering became the members of the royal court. In the 19th century special cards were printed which contained the names of the imagined courtiers and these cards would be dealt out to the party guests.

In some countries children are given presents on the Epiphany in memory of the gifts brought to the holy infant. In Germany the children carry a star around the villages to represent the star which guided the three kings.

The association with royalty continues in this country to the present day, for it is still the custom for the reigning monarch or representatives to take part in a ceremony in the chapel royal at St James's Palace, where the gifts of gold. frankincense and myrrh are offered to the clergy.

✵ Twelfth Night cake ✵

Traditionally a special cake was eaten on twelfth night.
Charms, money and sometimes a dry pea and bean were put into the
cake mixture as in a Christmas pudding. The person finding
the bean becomes King or Queen of the party and the recipient of
the pea becomes their consort.

For the cake:

400g flour
15g baking powder
pinch of salt
grated nutmeg
225g butter
225g caster sugar
4 eggs
400g currants
115g mixed peel
55g chopped almonds
6 tablespoons of brandy
1 dried pea
1 dried bean

1 Cream the butter and sugar together. Gradually beat in the eggs and add the rest of the ingredients.

2 Grease and line a cake tin. Bake in a pre-heated oven (gas mark 3 or 140 degrees C) for about three hours.

3 At the end of this time, keep the cake in the oven for thirty minutes with the heat off. Remove the cake from the tin and allow it to cool.

✤ Planting mistletoe berries ✤

Here is a way of ensuring that you have plenty of mistletoe for future Christmas decorations. Use a sharp knife to cut small flaps of bark under the branches of a tree. Place a mistletoe berry under each flap.

Pine needle bath oil

Pine needles don't necessarily have to be a nuisance.

1 Half fill a screw top jam jar with pine needles from your tree. Add 1 teaspoon of vodka and fill the rest of the jar with corn oil.

2 Shake the jar well every day for a week, then strain the contents and use the oil in your bath.

❧ Christmas cards ❧

Don't throw away your old Christmas cards. There are several ways of using them.

1 Make a Christmas card picture scrap book or a Christmas collage.

2 Make a Christmas treasure box. Cut out lots of shapes and pictures from the cards. Stick them all over a shoe box and when the box is dry coat it with a layer of varnish.

3 Cut up large pictures from the cards and make jigsaws.

4 Use pinking shears to cut out some picture tags for next year's gifts.

5 Mount the prettiest pictures on new sheets of folded card and use the new cards as "Thank you for my Christmas present" letters.

6 Cut out pairs of pictures. For example two scenes with robins on, two with reindeer, two with Santa etc. Shuffle the pictures, turn them face down and take turns at trying to find a similar pair. The winner is the one with the most pairs of cards.

✖ Thankyou letters ✖

After all the presents and the feasts and the parties have finished there is usually time to write thankyou letters. Children often have to be persuaded to do this, but if you suggest that they make code-word thank-you letters, they might be just a little more willing to sit down with pencil and paper.

The illustration on this page might give you a few ideas on how to begin.